Gay Issues and Politics: Marriage, the Military, & Work Place Discrimination

The Gallup's Guide to Modern Gay, Lesbian, & Transgender Lifestyle

Gay Issues and Politics: Marriage, the Military, & Work Place Discrimination

by Jaime A. Seba

Mason Crest Publishers

MASON CREST PUBLISHERS INC.
370 Reed Road
Broomall, Pennsylvania 19008
(866)MCP-BOOK (toll free)
www.masoncrest.com

First Printing
9 8 7 6 5 4 3 2 1

Library of Congress Cataloging-in-Publication Data
Seba, Jaime.
  Gay issues and politics : marriage, the military, & work place discrimination / by Jaime A. Seba.
      p. cm.— (The Gallup's guide to modern gay, lesbian, & transgender lifestyle)
  Includes bibliographical references and index.
  ISBN 978-1-4222-1750-4   ISBN 978-1-4222-1758-0 (series)
  ISBN 978-1-4222-1869-3 (pbk.)   ISBN 978-1-4222-1863-1 (series pbk.)

  1. Homosexuality—United States. 2. Discrimination—United States. I. Title.
  HQ75.16.U6S43 2011
  306.76'6—dc22
                                    2010012748

Produced by Harding House Publishing Service, Inc.
www.hardinghousepages.com
Interior design by MK Bassett-Harvey.
Cover design by Torque Advertising + Design.
Printed in the USA by Bang Printing

PICTURE CREDITS

Creative Commons: pp.11, 15, 16, 28, 30, 41, 45
Keys, Jere; Creative Commons: p. 58
Lahusen, Kay Tobin; Rainbow History: p. 53

Nozell, Marc; Creative Commons: p. 49
Terwilliger, Jessie; Creative Commons: p. 36
U.S. Congress: p. 56
U.S. National Institutes of Health: p. 21

Contents

Introduction

We are both individuals and community members. Our differences define individuality; our commonalities create a community. Some differences, like the ability to run swiftly or to speak confidently, can make an individual stand out in a way that is viewed as beneficial by a community, while the group may frown upon others. Some of those differences may be difficult to hide (like skin color or physical disability), while others can be hidden (like religious views or sexual orientation). Moreover, what some communities or cultures deem as desirable differences, like thinness, is a negative quality in other contemporary communities. This is certainly the case with sexual orientation and gender identity, as explained in *Homosexuality Around the World*, one of the volumes in this book series.

Often, there is a tension between the individual (individual rights) and the community (common good). This is easily visible in everyday matters like the right to own land versus the common good of building roads. These cases sometimes result in community controversy and often are adjudicated by the courts.

An even more basic right than property ownership, however, is one's gender and sexuality. Does the right of gender expression trump the concerns and fears of a community or a family or a school? *Feeling Wrong in Your Own Body*, as the author of that volume suggests, means confronting, in the most personal way, the tension between individuality and community. And, while a community, family, and school have the right (and obligation) to protect its children, does the notion of property rights extend to controlling young adults' choice as to how they express themselves in terms of gender or sexuality?

Changes in how a community (or a majority of the community) thinks about an individual right or responsibility often precedes changes in the law enacted by legislatures or decided by courts. And for these changes to occur, individuals (sometimes working in small groups) often defied popular opinion, political pressure, or religious beliefs. Some of these trends are discussed in *A New Generation of Homosexuality*. Every generation (including yours!) stands on the accomplishments of our ancestors and in *Gay and Lesbian Role Models* you'll be reading about some of them.

One of the most pernicious aspects of discrimination on the basis of sexual orientation is that "homosexuality" is a stigma that can be hidden (see the volume about *Homophobia*). While some of my generation (I was your age in the early 1960s) think that life is so much easier being "queer" in the age of the Internet, Gay-Straight Alliances, and Ellen, in reality, being different in areas where difference matters is *always* difficult. Coming Out, as described in the volume of the same title, is always challenging—for both those who choose to come out and for the friends and family they trust with what was once a hidden truth. Being healthy means being honest—at least to yourself. Having supportive friends and family is most important, as explained in *Being Gay, Staying Healthy*.

Sometimes we create our own "families"—persons bound together by love and identity but not by name or bloodline. This is quite common in gay communities today as it was several generations ago. Forming families or small communities based on rejection by the larger community can also be a double-edged sword. While these can be positive, they may also turn into prisons of conformity. Does being lesbian, for example, mean everyone has short hair, hates men, and drives (or rides on) a motorcycle? *What Does It Mean to Be Gay, Lesbian, Bisexual, or Transgender?* "smashes" these and other stereotypes.

Another common misconception is that "all gay people are alike"—a classic example of a stereotypical statement. We may be drawn together because of a common prejudice or oppression, but we should not forfeit our individuality for the sake of the safety of a common identity, which is one of the challenges shown in *Gay People of Color: Facing Prejudices, Forging Identities*.

Coming out to who *you* are is just as important as having a group or "family" within which to safely come out. Becoming knowledgeable about these issues (through the books in this series and the other resources to which they will lead), feeling good about yourself, behaving safely, actively listening to others *and* to your inner spirit—all this will allow you to fulfill your promise and potential.

James T. Sears, PhD
Consultant

chapter 1

The History of Identity Politics

As Adrienne Hudek explored the United States Holocaust Memorial Museum, she was moved by the many displays about the horrors suffered by Jewish people. Then she saw a display about Nazi persecution of homosexuals from 1933 to 1945. As she stood and read the details of how thousands of gay people were murdered, she was shocked.

"That's something people don't talk about so much," she said. "I can't believe that ever happened. But it's important for us to remember that it did, so we can stop these things from happening again."

Today popular culture is full of positive gay icons such as musician Sir Elton John and television host Ellen DeGeneres. Rainbow-colored displays celebrate gay pride across the country during annual festivals. And with access to a diverse collection of viewpoints and information on the Internet, people are becoming increasingly familiar with gay issues and their relationship to national politics.

EXTRA INFO

The Holocaust is the term generally used to describe the Nazi slaughter of approximately six million European Jews during World War II. The word comes from a Greek term that means "sacrifice by fire." People often forget, though, that the Holocaust also included the Nazis' systematic murder of millions of people in other groups, including ethnic Poles, Romani (gypsies), Soviet civilians, Soviet prisoners of war, people with disabilities, Jehovah's Witnesses—and homosexuals. With these numbers included, the Holocaust's victims climb to between 11 million and 17 million people.

Between 5,000 and 15,000 German homosexuals were sent to concentration camps. The Nazi government declared that homosexuals were contrary to "wholesome popular sentiment," and homosexuals were consequently regarded as "defilers of German blood." The Gestapo (the Nazi police) raided gay bars, tracked individuals using the address books of those they arrested, used the subscription lists of gay magazines to find others, and encouraged people to scrutinize the behavior of their neighbors and report suspected homosexual behaviors. Tens of thousands gays were convicted between 1933 and 1944 and sent to camps for "rehabilitation," where they were identified first by yellow armbands and later by pink triangles worn on the left side of the jacket and the right pants leg. Hundreds were castrated by court order; others were humiliated, tortured, used in hormone experiments conducted by Nazi doctors, and killed.

After the war, the full extent of gay suffering was slow to come out. Many victims kept their stories to themselves because homosexuality remained a criminal offense in postwar Germany.

But these positive images are just part of the most recent chapter in the evolution of gay equality. For centuries, some have used the Bible as a weapon again homosexuals. Even today, despite more acceptance and understanding, the fight for gay rights continues every day in the United States and around the world. In some places, including Saudi Arabia and Iran, homosexuality is punishable by imprisonment and even death.

Understanding the history of gay issues begins with something as simple as defining the term "homosexual." While today it commonly refers to sexual

During the Holocaust, the German Gestapo dragged people from their homes and arrested them, including Jews, homosexuals, and Roma.

attraction to people of one's own sex, the meaning has changed significantly over time.

The word "homosexual" rarely appeared in print until 1926, when the *New York Times* became the first major American publication to use term. At that time, homosexuality was considered a medical disorder or mental illness. Young people who acted upon or even merely acknowledged homosexual feelings were often placed in institutions and subjected to horrific medical treatments in an attempt to "cure" the illness.

But as time moved forward, experts began to speak out about these practices. In 1935, noted psychiatrist Sigmund Freud wrote in a letter that homosexuality "is nothing to be ashamed of, no vice, no degradation, it cannot be classified as an illness . . . it is a great injustice to persecute homosexuality as a crime." This statement was later reprinted in the *American Journal of Psychiatry* in 1951.

Still, it took another twenty-two years before the Board of Directors of the American Psychiatric Association removed "homosexuality" from its *Diagnostic and Statistical Manual of Mental Disorders* (DSM). But it

What's That Mean?

Bigotry is the stubborn and complete intolerance of any religion, appearance, belief, or ethnic background that differs from one's own.

was replaced with another variation on the diagnosis, called ego-dystonic homosexuality, which wasn't removed entirely from the DSM until 1986.

Regardless of definitions and medical terms, though, *bigotry* continued much closer to home for gay people, especially young men and women who heard in their schools, churches, and even their homes that being gay was wrong, a disease, and something of which to be ashamed. Numerous organizations even exist to "cure" individuals of homosexuality, including Exodus International. The nonprofit Christian organization, formed in the 1970s, claims to offer freedom from homosexuality through the power of Jesus Christ. JONAH is a Jewish organization that claims to use psychological techniques to free "strugglers" from homosexual desires.

EXTRA INFO

The African-American Civil Rights Movement was at a peak between 1955 and1965. Martin Luther King Jr., among others, led the fight to change American laws and attitudes. As a result of their efforts, Congress passed the Civil Rights Act of 1964 and the Voting Rights Act of 1965, guaranteeing basic civil rights for all Americans, regardless of race, after nearly a decade of nonviolent protests and marches, ranging from the 1955–1956 Montgomery bus boycott to the student-led sit-ins of the 1960s to the huge March on Washington in 1963.

Considering this complicated and often shaming history, it's understandable that the gay rights movement didn't begin until the 1960s. After years of public protests and increasing debate over equal rights, the movement finally took shape in 1969 with what would later be known as the Stonewall Riots.

The riots began after a police raid on June 28, 1969 at the Stonewall Inn, a gay bar in Greenwich Village in New York City. Known as one of the few gay-friendly areas of New York City, Greenwich Village was often considered a safe haven for individuals looking to meet and socialize with other gay people, without fear of reprisal or attack. Or, at least, there was less fear.

EXTRA INFO

The offices of shadow U.S. Representative and shadow U.S. Senator are elected by the voters of the six U.S. Territories and the District of Columbia as part of their efforts to gain full admittance to the Union as States. The voters of the District of Columbia elect two shadow senators who are known as U.S. senators by the District of Columbia, but who are not officially sworn in or seated by the U.S. Senate. Shadow senators were first elected in 1990.

At that time, police raids on gay bars were common. But with the growing force of the African-American Civil Rights Movement and anti-war demonstrations, people were becoming increasingly empowered to stand up for equal rights and fair treatment.

"Stonewall is the beginning of a true movement where we said, 'I will not let you harass, beat, and arrest me just because you don't like me.' Of the big things that happened in 1969, such as the moon landing, Stonewall is remembered," said Sabrina Sojourner, who became the first openly lesbian African-American to hold the title of U.S. Representative when she was elected as the "shadow" representative from the District of Columbia. "It could have been forgotten. Instead, it inspired generations."

Early in the morning, police officers slammed through the doors of the Stonewall Inn, shouting for the two hundred patrons inside to line up to have identification checked. Instead, the people in the bar refused. Frustrated at the injustice of being harassed simply for being gay, they began to protest. Soon, dozens more people joined in from the street. As the crowd grew more and more restless, seeing their only outlet for

Sabrina Sojourner represented three minority groups—blacks, women, and lesbians—when she was elected to the House of Representatives.

personal expression threatened, police quickly lost control of the situation. The *Daily News* featured the headline "3 Cops Hurt as Bar Raid Riles Crowd" and included this information, buried on page 30:

A predawn police raid on a reputed Greenwich Village homosexual hangout, the second raid within a week, touched off a two-hour melee yesterday as customers and villagers swarmed

Today, the Stonewall Inn in New York City is a symbol of pride for the gay community.

over the plainclothes cops. Before order was restored, the cops were the targets of thrown coins, cobblestones and uprooted parking meters, windows were smashed, a police van was nearly overturned and the front of the raided bar, the Stonewall Inn, was fire-bombed.

Rioting and protesting carried over into the next evening, as thousands of people turned up to support the first major event of the gay rights movement.

"Before Stonewall, you took your life in your hands when you tried to be openly gay," recalls Martin Duberman, author of the book *Stonewall*. "Whenever we celebrate pride, a component of that pride should be that we are proud of our history and struggle and (that we) fought back against oppression and managed to have lives under that difficulty."

On the first anniversary of the riots, that feeling was embodied in the country's first Gay Pride march. The event, which was held in Greenwich Village, filled fifteen city blocks with peaceful marchers carrying signs and banners. Similar marches were held in Los Angeles and Chicago at the same time.

The following year, numerous cities joined in the celebration that now continues annually around the globe. Gay pride parades became festivals highlighted with musical performances and speeches from activists and civil rights leaders. Families and supporters of the gay community join in to celebrate diversity with banners, costumes, and colorful balloons. All of this came from the ruins of that groundbreaking day at the Stonewall Inn.

But as with all steps forward, these events also draw protests from religious and political **conservatives**, enraged at such a positive celebration of gay rights.

As the gay rights movement continued to grow, gay people became increasingly aware of the need for representation in politics. Openly gay politician Harvey Milk took the first steps in 1977, when he was elected to the San Francisco Board of Supervisors. By 1980, a political action committee called the Human Rights Campaign (HRC) was formed to raise money for congressional candidates who supported fairness to the gay community. The organization grew to being one of the largest lesbian, gay, bisexual, and *transgender* civil rights *advocacy* groups in the United States.

In response to the growing demand for equal rights, anti-gay *activists* such as singer Anita Bryant increasingly spoke out against homosexuality. As the leader of a group called Save Our Children, often considered the country's first national anti-gay group, Bryant frequently campaigned to strip away the limited rights and protections granted to the gay community. These movements led to her name being permanently linked with hatred, bigotry, and *homophobia*. At that same time, author James Dobson founded Focus on the Family, which grew to be America's wealthiest *fundamentalist* ministry and later led the movement against gay marriage. Other vocal opponents of gay rights included

What's That Mean?

Advocacy is the act of standing up on behalf of someone or something.

Activists are people who take direct action in support of a cause or belief.

Homophobia is fear and dislike of gay people.

Someone who is a *fundamentalist* belongs to a religious movement that believes in that religion's fundamental principles and follows them rigidly, often combined with intolerance of other views. When the word is used in connection with Christianity, it refers to a member of a form of Protestant Christianity that believes in the strict and literal interpretation of the Bible.

Reverend Jerry Falwell, founder of the Moral Majority, and Pat Buchanan, the communications director for President Ronald Reagan, who claimed that AIDS was "nature's revenge on gay men."

But perhaps the most significant political event to impact the gay rights movement was the AIDS *epidemic* that darkened the 1980s. Beginning as an illness found only in gay men in the late 1970s, it was originally called "gay cancer" or GRID (gay-related immune deficiency). This name immediately linked homosexuality with a deadly disease. Numerous doctors, researchers, politicians, and historians have agreed that this public perception caused the illness to be misunderstood by most of the American population. Even worse, religious *extremists* used the illness as evidence of punishment of the gay lifestyle, fanning the flames of fear and uncertainty that were sweeping the nation. As a result, more focus was placed on the epidemic as a gay issue than as a medical issue, causing a severe delay in proper education about prevention and self-protection.

What's That Mean?

An *epidemic* is a widespread outbreak of a disease.

Extremists are people who are in favor of using extreme measures (taking action beyond normal measures), especially in politics and religion.

The medical community, though, recognized that the condition was not limited to homosexuals. In 1982, after more than 200 U.S. cases had been reported, the Centers for Disease Control officially recognized it as AIDS, the acquired immune deficiency syndrome. Still, President Ronald Reagan did not use the term "AIDS" in public until September

In 1987, President Ronald Reagan met with HHS Secretary Otis R. Bowen, Dr. James B. Wyngaarden, and members of the Commission on the Human Immunodeficiency Virus (HIV) Epidemic. In his remarks, the president said, "I hope the commission will help us all put aside our suspicions and work together with common sense against this threat." Members of the gay community felt the president would have responded more quickly and strongly against a similar threat to the straight community.

17, 1985, when he announced funding would be provided for AIDS research. At that time, more than 5,500 deaths had already been identified in the U.S.

More than thirty years after the beginning of the epidemic, the Kaiser Family Foundation estimates that more than 580,000 people have died in the United States, where more than 1.7 million people have been infected with HIV (human immunodeficiency virus), the virus that causes AIDS. In 1987, the book *And the Band Played On: Politics, People and the AIDS Epidemic* by journalist Randy Shilts directly attributed the rapid spread of AIDS in America to the mistreatment of the gay community, both by legislative officials and the medical community, which delayed a proper and **proactive** response. The book received high critical acclaim and quickly became a bestseller

"The numbers of AIDS cases measured the shame of the nation," Shilts wrote. "The United States, the one nation with the knowledge, the resources, and the institutions to respond to the epidemic, had failed. And it failed because of ignorance and fear, prejudice and rejection. The story of the AIDS epidemic was that simple . . . it was a story of bigotry and what it could do to a nation."

What's That Mean?

Proactive means acting in advance to deal with an expected difficulty.

EXTRA INFO

Hate crimes occur when a perpetrator targets a victim because of his or her membership in a certain social group, usually a racial group, religion, sexual orientation, disability, nationality, age, or gender identity. The term usually refers to criminal acts motivated by hatred. The crimes include physical assault, damage to property, bullying, harassment, verbal abuse or insults, offensive graffiti, or hate mail.

Policymakers in many nations and at all levels of government have become more concerned about hate crimes in recent years, but these crimes are not new. The Romans persecuted the early Christians; the Ottomans slaughtered the Armenians; the Nazis sent millions of Jews and others to the crematoriums; and more recently, the world was horrified by the ethnic cleansing in Bosnia and the genocide in Rwanda. Hate crimes have shaped the world's history.

In the United States, racial and religious prejudice has inspired most hate crimes. As Europeans began to colonize the New World in the sixteenth and seventeenth centuries, Native tribes increasingly became the targets of intimidation and violence. After the Civil War, African Americans were lynched by the Ku Klux Klan and other hate groups. The Klan's hate targets included lesbian, gay, bisexual, and transgender people.

Despite the scientific medical evidence proving that AIDS was by no means limited to homosexuals, the initial connection between AIDS/HIV and the gay community all but halted the advancement of social equality.

But from this dark time in American history emerged some notable organizations that have had a significant impact on gay issues and politics. The Gay and Lesbian Alliance Against Defamation (GLAAD) was formed in 1985 to protest the *New York Post*'s coverage of the epidemic. Since then, the organization has played a large role in changing the way the gay community is portrayed in media and entertainment.

As these organizations continued to form, the gay community developed more of a voice in politics, enabling local state and national groups to respond to growing issues such as hate crimes, homophobia, marriage equality, workplace discrimination, and the military's "Don't ask, Don't tell" policy regarding gay people serving in the U.S. armed forces. Using

EXTRA INFO

Harvey Milk was murdered on November 27, 1978, by an enraged political adversary who had spoken openly against homosexuality and gay rights.

grassroots movements and online information sharing, growing numbers of gay community members and supporters continue to speak out to achieve equal rights.

These groups took center stage when the horrific torture and murder of Matthew Shepard captured headlines across the country and brought homophobia back into the spotlight. Shepard, a twenty-one-year-old student at the University of Wyoming, was offered a ride late one night in October 1998. After admitting he was gay, he was brutally beaten and murdered, then roped to a fence and left on a deserted road to die. News of the attack swept the nation, prompting candlelight vigils and prayer sessions as Shepard struggled to survive in intensive care. He died on October 12, 1998, five days after the attack. In the aftermath, Shepard became a national symbol of the need for tolerance among young people.

What's That Mean?

Grassroots refers to people or society at a local level rather than at the center of major political activity.

"I would like to see every gay doctor come out, every gay lawyer, every gay architect come out, stand up and let the world know. That would do more to end prejudice overnight than anybody would imagine," Harvey Milk said in a tape recording to be played in the event of his assassination. "I urge them to do that, urge them to come out. Only that way will we start to achieve our rights."

FIND OUT MORE ON THE INTERNET

The American Gay Rights Movement: A Short History
civilliberty.about.com/od/gendersexuality/tp/History-Gay-Rights-Movement.htm

The American Gay Rights Movement: A Timeline
www.infoplease.com/ipa/A0761909.html

READ MORE ABOUT IT

Carter, David. Stonewall: *The Riots That Sparked the Gay Revolution*. New York: St. Martin's Griffin, 2005.

Marcus, Eric. *Making Gay History: The Half-Century Fight for Lesbian and Gay Equal Rights*. New York: Harper, 2002.

Miller, Neil. *Out of the Past: Gay and Lesbian History.* New York: Advocate, 2008.

chapter 2

Same-Sex Marriage

Just like most grooms, Rob Kelly was nervous on his wedding day. Friends had come in from out of town, and he wanted everything to go right. As his sisters helped him get ready for the most important day of his life, he looked in the mirror over and over again, fixing his hair and making sure he looked perfect. He took a deep breath, thought of spending his future with his best friend, and made the happy and joyful walk down the aisle.

The ceremony had it all, vows, a minister, flowers, friends and family, matching rings, and most important, a couple in love. The only thing missing was the marriage license.

"We had a wedding with gifts and a reception, the whole thing," said Kelly, who had a marriage ceremony with his partner Sean in 2007. The wedding was not considered a legal union, however, because New York State doesn't recognize gay marriage. "I don't see how anyone can tell us we're not married, especially when it means that we don't get the same rights as straight couples."

But the United States government can. This is because of the Defense of Marriage Act (DOMA), which was signed into law by President Bill Clinton in 1996. DOMA holds that no state must honor same-sex marriages from other states, and that the federal

LAWS REGARDING SAME-SEX PARTNERSHIPS IN THE UNITED STATES

- Same-sex marriage
- Unions granting rights similar to marriage
- Legislation granting limited/enumerated rights
- Same-sex marriages performed elsewhere recognized
- No specific prohibition or recognition of same-sex marriages or unions
- Statute bans same-sex marriage
- Constitution bans same-sex marriage
- Constitution bans same-sex marriage and other kinds of same-sex unions

Laws regarding same-sex partnerships in the United States as of December 2009.

government has defined marriage as being a legal union between only one man and one woman.

According to the Human Rights Campaign, barring same-sex couples from federally recognized marriage denies them hundreds of basic protections and rights given to married heterosexual couples, including hospital visitation, Social Security benefits, immigration, health insurance, family leave, and pensions.

When Kenneth Johnson's partner James was rushed to the emergency room, Ken desperately sought information from the hospital staff. But they would only give information to immediate family. Even though they were registered as domestic partners in the state of California, he was told that he was "just a friend."

"At our covenant ceremony," Ken said. "I took James to be my life partner, 'for better for worse, for richer for poorer, in sickness and in health, to love and to cherish, until we are parted by death.' At the ceremony, I promised James: "I'm not leaving, no matter what."

But he had to leave, to make the nearly three-hour drive home and back to get the documentation showing that James had given him power of attorney. Fortunately, he returned in time to spend precious last minutes with his husband, who died the following day. This is just one of thousands of examples of what is lost when committed partners are not legally recognized.

The fight for same-sex marriage began decades earlier, when University of Minnesota students Jack Baker and James Michael McConnell applied for a marriage license in Hennepin County, Minnesota, in 1970. After the court clerk denied their request, they sued in District Court. And lost. They appealed to the State Supreme Court, and lost. They even took the case to the U.S. Supreme Court, but were dismissed.

These are widely recognized as the first legal battles over the issue of same-sex marriage. And they were

San Francisco mayor Gavin Newsom, shown here participating in a Gay Pride parade, has been an outspoken supporter of marriage equality for homosexuals.

hardly the last. The years before and after DOMA saw a series of lawsuits, legal maneuvers, and court decisions aimed at determining each state's stance on gay marriage.

On Valentine's Day 2001, the organization Marriage Equality USA organized same-sex couples in Los Angeles, New York City, and San Francisco to apply for marriage licenses. All were declined. But San Francisco Mayor Gavin Newsom breathed new life into the movement in 2004, when he began issuing the country's first marriage certificates to same-sex couples. As a home to the nation's counter-culture since the 1950s, San Francisco had stood out as the center of the gay rights movement since creation of the urban gay neighborhood the Castro and the election of openly gay activist Harvey Milk to the Board of Supervisors in the 1970s.

Although the California Supreme Court later **nullified** the San Francisco marriage licenses, the trend continued that same year when Massachusetts became the first U.S. state to legalize same-sex marriage.

By 2007, New Hampshire, Oregon, and Washington advanced equality in their states by allowing forms of civil unions or domestic partnerships for gay couples. The next year, the Supreme Courts of

California and Connecticut also recognized same-sex marriage, and in 2009, Iowa, Vermont, Maine, and New Hampshire legalized same-sex marriage, too. In 2010, same-sex marriages were recognized in the District of Columbia.

The decision by the California Supreme Court that same-sex marriage was legal under the state constitution gained national attention when thousands of couples were wed, including comedian Ellen DeGeneres and her partner, actress Portia de Rossi.

But the ruling of the Supreme Court doesn't always reflect the will of the people. The decision stirred up **controversy** throughout California and across the country. Heated debates began, and groups claiming the need to protect families launched a campaign in support of Proposition 8. This measure, also known as the California Marriage Protection Act, stated that "only marriage between a man and a woman is valid or recognized in California." Less than five months—and thousands of weddings—after the Supreme Court's decision, California voters passed Proposition 8 on Election Day, November 2008. Same-sex marriage was no longer legal in the state of California.

What's That Mean?

A *controversy* is a dispute, argument, or debate, especially one concerning a matter about which there is strong disagreement and especially one that is carried on in public or in the press.

EXTRA INFO

Civil unions and domestic partnerships are not the same thing as marriage. What's the difference?

Marriage establishes a legal kinship between two people. It is a relationship that is recognized across cultures, countries, and religions. Civil unions and domestic partnerships, however, are often not recognized outside of the state where they were issued (and only some states allow them). Here are some other differences:

- A United States citizen who is married can sponsor his or her non-American spouse for immigration into this country. Those with civil unions or domestic partnerships have no such privilege.
- Civil unions and domestic partnerships are not recognized by the federal government, so couples cannot file joint-tax returns or be eligible for tax breaks or protections the government affords to married couples.
- The General Accounting Office in 1997 released a list of 1,049 benefits and protections available to heterosexual married couples, ranging from benefits such as survivor benefits, veteran benefits, and Social Security to sick leave to care for an ailing partner and insurance breaks. They also include things like family discounts, obtaining family insurance through your employer, visiting your spouse in the hospital, and making medical decisions if your partner is unable. Civil unions protect some of these rights but not all of them.

"It (is) the first time in history that they would change the state constitution and take rights away. It's just amazing," DeGeneres said on her popular daytime talk show following the election that also saw the United States elect its first African-American president, Barack Obama. "Here we're taking a giant step towards equality and then this is happening, and I don't understand it."

EXTRA INFO

We usually think of democracy as a form of government where the majority rules. That definition has been used to vote down proposals for same-sex marriage. But the founders of our country worried that the majority could abuse its powers to oppress a minority just as easily as a king could. So they set up the Bill of Rights to protect the rights of all Americans, including minorities.

During the African-American Civil Rights Movement, blacks were the minority in the United States. If it came down to a vote between blacks and whites, whites would always win. In the early twentieth century, however, some black leaders adopted a strategy of nonviolence and civil disobedience that took full advantage of the freedoms contained in the Bill of Rights. By doing so, they challenged America to live up to its legal foundations. They demanded legal equality and justice in the courts, forcing Americans to extend rights to the minority.

But California was not alone in taking a step back on the issue of gay civil rights that year. Arizona and Florida voters also chose to outlaw same-sex marriage, bringing the total to thirty states that had passed bans on gay marriage.

Considering California's historically *liberal* leanings, with diverse cultural centers such as San Francisco and Los Angeles, the show of intolerance was especially surprising. In a statement responding to the Proposition 8 vote in California, actor George Clooney said: "At some point in our lifetime, gay marriage won't be an issue, and everyone who stood against the civil right will look as outdated as George Wallace standing on the school steps keeping James Hood from entering the University of Alabama because he was black."

Many gay rights activists drew similar parallels to the black civil rights movements of the 1960s, when popular opinion was outweighed by the rule of Supreme Court. Ironically, though, the increased turnout of minority voters for the presidential election is thought to have sealed the fate of gay marriage in California, where exit polls showed that 70 percent of black voters supported the ban.

What's That Mean?

Someone who is *liberal* is open to change and new ideas.

"We got married just a few days before Election Day, because we knew Prop 8 would pass," said Tom Brinkley, who married his partner in California in 2008. "I know there are people out there who don't understand gay marriage or who think it's a threat. But people felt the same way about interracial couples getting married forty years ago. If we'd listened to those people, just think what the world would be like today."

U.S. Congressman John Lewis, who participated in the 1963 March on Washington led by Dr. Martin Luther King, is among many civil rights leaders who see the similarities in the struggle for gay rights. He has frequently spoken out about the need for the

Many people were taken by surprise when so many people in seemingly liberal California were so strongly against gay marriage that Preposition 8 passed in 2009, making same-sex marriage no longer legal in that state.

EXTRA INFO

Evangelical Christians against same-sex marriages are convinced that homosexuality is a sin. Here is a summary of their perspectives, written by Christian Family Law Association:

If we assume, for the sake of argument, that a person could have a gene that produces a tendency toward a particular behavior, does the presence of such a genetic tendency justify the behavior? One might argue that God made me that way, and since he does not make mistakes, he must have intended that I act in accordance with my genetic tendency. But such a view ignores what the Bible has to say about man's fallen and sinful nature. It also ignores the idea that there are absolute moral truths that have governed society and behaviors since ancient times. Basing our laws on [genetic tendencies] would mean that we should accept all forms of greed, pedophilia, sadomasochism, and other destructive behaviors to which people can be genetically inclined. Our innate desires or tendencies, even genetic tendencies, must not be confused with God's will for our identities to be moral, righteous, and consistent with biblical truth. An innate desire or tendency may be morally appropriate and lawful in one context, yet highly immoral and unlawful in another. For instance, an innate tendency for sexual arousal with a spouse is considered morally appropriate and lawful, while sexual arousal with a child is not only immoral but criminal. We can conclude that although we are not morally responsible for having a particular genetic tendency or desire, we are morally responsible for what we act on and do.

(From "A Christian Perspective on Same-Sex Relationships," www.christianfamilylawassociation.org/same-sex_relationships)

same rights and equalities he fought for in the 1960s to be extended to the gay community.

"We cannot keep turning our backs on gay and lesbian Americans. I have fought too hard and too long against discrimination based on race and color not to stand up against discrimination based on sexual orientation," Congressman Lewis said in 2003. "I've heard the reasons for opposing civil marriage for same-sex couples. Cut through the distractions, and they stink of the same fear, hatred, and intolerance I have known in racism and bigotry."

Despite the resistance, gay rights continue to push forward around the world. The couples who were married in California before Proposition 8 was passed are still married under California law. And gay marriage, domestic partnerships, or civil unions are legal in numerous parts of the globe, including Mexico, Finland, Holland, Germany, Canada, South Africa, New Zealand, Israel, the United Kingdom, Vietnam, Sweden, Portugal, Argentina, Hungary, Norway, Uruguay, Switzerland, and the Czech Republic.

"We have a lot of work to do in our common struggle against bigotry and discrimination," said Coretta Scott King, civil rights activist and widow of Dr. Martin Luther King, Jr. "I say 'common struggle,' because I believe very strongly that all forms of bigotry and discrimination are equally wrong and should be opposed by right-thinking Americans everywhere. Freedom from discrimination based on sexual orientation is surely a fundamental human right in any great democracy, as much as freedom from racial, religious, gender, or ethnic discrimination."

FIND OUT MORE ON THE INTERNET

History of Gay Marriage
yesongaymarriage.com/why_yes/history_of_gay_marriage/

Time's Brief History of Gay Marriage
www.time.com/time/magazine/article/0,9171,1808617,00.html

Two Perspectives on Gay Marriage
pewresearch.org/pubs/820/two-perspectives-on-gay-marriage

READ MORE ABOUT IT

Baird, Robert M. and Stuart E. Townsend, eds. *Same-Sex Marriage: The Moral and Legal Debate.* Amherst, N.Y.: Prometheus, 2004.

Gerstmann, Evan. *Same-Sex Marriage and the Constitution.* New York: Cambridge University Press, 2008.

Sullivan, Andrew. *Same-Sex Marriage: Pro and Con.* New York: Vintage, 2004. Amherst, N.Y.: Prometheus, 2004.

chapter 3

Gays in the Military

Historic Congressional Cemetery in Washington, D.C., is the final resting place of nearly a hundred senators and representatives, as well as American patriots such as FBI Director J. Edgar Hoover. Among those notable memorials is a black stone marker that bears no name. Instead it reads: "When I was in the military they gave me a medal for killing two men and a discharge for loving one."

This is the grave of Leonard P. Matlovich, who served as a technical sergeant in the United States Air Force during the Vietnam War. He was awarded the Purple Heart and the Bronze Star. He taught Air Force Race Relations classes.

And he was gay.

Matlovich made headlines when he challenged the military's ban on homosexuals serving in the military. On Memorial Day in 1975, his personal battle became public knowledge with an article in the *New York Times* and a television interview with Walter Cronkite. On September 8, 1975, Matlovich appeared on the cover of *Time* magazine, accompanied by the declaration, "I am a homosexual."

The Air Force offered him the chance to remain in the military, provided he would sign a statement pledging to never practice homosexuality again. Matlovich refused. He sued for reinstatement but eventually settled when he believed it was clear that the conservative U.S. Supreme Court would deny his appeal. Instead, Matlovich dedicated his life to the gay rights movement.

"I found myself, little nobody me, standing up in front of tens of thousands of gay people," he told *Time*. "And just two years ago I thought I was the

Nations that do not bar openly homosexual people from serving in the military
Nations with semi-ambiguous policies ("don't ask, don't tell," etc.)
Nations with a ban on homosexual people in the military

Not all countries ban gays from serving in the military. This map shows the status for homosexuals in the military in nations around the world as of October 2009.

only gay in the world. It was a mixture of joy and sadness. It was just great pride to be an American, to know I'm oppressed but able to stand up there and say so."

The groundbreaking case brought the issue of gay men and women serving in the military into the spotlight. But some historians believe the issue took root centuries earlier, when homosexuals were dismissed from the U.S. military as far back as the Revolutionary War. Since then, gay soldiers have been court-martialed and discharged, either honorably or dishonorably. Often the dismissal barred them from receiving benefits, continuing the discrimination into civilian life.

At the time of Matlovich's groundbreaking court case, the policy of the U.S. military was to ask new recruits about their sexual orientation before they were permitted to serve. If service members were gay, or even suspected of being gay, they could be prosecuted and imprisoned.

"I recall looking hard at the word 'homosexual' on the entry form I filled out to enlist in the U.S. Air Force, then at the 'Yes' or 'No' boxes that followed the word. It seemed as though time stood still as I considered how to answer that question," recalls Garland Auton, who joined the Air Force in 1987.

As time went on, I continued to be dedicated, hard working, and professional, but I also started to be more afraid of being discovered as a gay man in the military. As my enlistment neared its end, I had to make a decision on whether to stay in the military and continue being afraid of who I was or to receive an honorable discharge and move on. I made my decision after re-reading a section of the Declaration of Independence: 'that all men are created equal, that they are endowed by their Creator with certain unalienable Rights, that among these are Life, Liberty and the pursuit of Happiness.' In order to pursue my happiness, I could no longer serve in the military. I could not continue to live a double life.

Many gay activists were hopeful in 1992, when then-presidential candidate Bill Clinton stated publicly that he opposed the military's exclusion of gay, lesbian, and bisexual soldiers. Many hoped that the silence would finally come to an end, and all Americans could serve their country openly. After Clinton's election, national debate on the issue raged across the country. Gay rights advocates felt sexual orientation had no bearing on a person's ability to serve in the military. Hearings were held before the Senate Armed Services Committee, and the result was a compromise reached in 1993 that has come to be known as "Don't Ask, Don't Tell, Don't Pursue, Don't Harass."

The decision was far from a victory for gay rights. Although it prohibits recruiters and military authorities from asking about an individual's sexual orientation, it also states that gays and lesbians can be discharged for making statements about their sexuality, either in public or in private, attempting to marry someone of the same sex, or if they are caught engaging in a homosexual act.

What's That Mean?

Empirical evidence is factual data gathered from direct observation.

"The policy is an absurdity and borderlines on being an obscenity," said Clifford Alexander, Former Secretary of the Army.

> What it does is cause people to ask of themselves that they lie to themselves, that they pretend to be something that they are not. There is no *empirical evidence* that would indicate that it affects military cohesion. There is a lot of evidence to say that the biases of the past have been layered onto the United States Army.

More than 13,000 individuals have been discharged under the "Don't Ask, Don't Tell" policy, according to the Servicemembers' Legal Defense Network (SLDN), which estimates this has cost taxpayers more than a quarter of a billion dollars. Approximately one thousand of these individuals have been in highly necessary positions, including engineers and interpreters of Middle Eastern languages. Many of these men and women have since joined SLDN to fight the legal battle against this policy, including former U.S. Army Sergeant Darren Manzella. He served in the Combat Lifesaver program, training nonmedical soldiers in emergency first-aid procedures. While under fire in Iraq, he cared for injured soldiers and earned

To commemorate the 14th anniversary of the "Don't Ask, Don't Tell" law, the Human Rights Campaign displayed 12,000 flags on the National Mall to recognize the 12,000 men and women discharged from the military since the law's enactment.

a Combat Medical Badge. Manzella was also threatened with being outed as gay and investigated under "Don't Ask, Don't Tell." He wrote:

I don't think most people can understand how hard it is to have to hide their true self; to have to pretend to be someone that they are not; to be scared that you'll be **ostracized** for being different; to be told that you're wrong if you live a certain life . . . that concerns no one else but yourself. . . . I am proud of myself and of the accomplishments I have achieved in my life. I

EXTRA INFO

A 2000 Defense Department inspector general survey showed that 80 percent of service members had heard offensive speech, derogatory names, jokes, or remarks about gays in the previous year, and that 85 percent believed such comments were tolerated. Thirty-seven percent reported that they had witnessed or experienced direct, targeted forms of harassment, including verbal and physical assaults and property damage. Overwhelmingly, service members did not report the harassment. When asked why, many cited fear of retaliation.

know that being gay would not have made a difference in receiving my college degree . . . my time spent as a psychiatric counselor . . . [and] certainly didn't make a difference when I treated injuries and saved lives in the streets of Baghdad.

SLDN studies also found that young adults between the ages of eighteen and twenty-five are now the group most significantly impacted by this policy. In the Air Force in 2002, 83 percent of "Don't Ask, Don't Tell" discharges were in this age group.

Once such case involved Pfc. Barry Winchell, who died shortly before his twenty-second birthday after being attacked with a baseball bat in barracks at Fort Campbell, Kentucky. Witnesses reported that Winchell had been the victim of severe harassment and inquiries related to his sexuality. The incident occurred in 1999, six years after "Don't Ask, Don't Tell" was enacted. Such incidents were not uncommon.

"When I got out of the field and was released for the weekend, I walked to my truck and found a sign with 'FAG' written on it sitting on my windshield," said former Staff Sergeant Leonard Peacock, who served from 1995–2001.

It concerned me, but I threw it away because I didn't want to attract attention. But the harassment didn't stop there. I got to my truck one day to see black stickers spelling out, "FAG," "RAINBOW WARRIOR," "GAY" and other *epithets* on my windshield. This experience in my new unit began to sour me on the military — there were so many people basing their judgments of me on *stereotypes*.

I would have enjoyed continuing my service, if we were all just treated equally. As it was, I put in more than six years. Being mistreated by so many other soldiers and being discharged from the military just because of one's sexual orientation is discrimination — plain and simple. I do not understand how our society allows it to happen, if we are all so advanced and civilized. What makes gay, lesbian, and bisexual soldiers different? We are not different; we all fight as soldiers. We all put our lives on the line, fighting for the same cause.

Another major flaw in the policy is the lack of confidential recourses for gays and lesbians who continue to serve in the military. In other words, they don't have anyone they can talk to without worrying that what they say will be reported. Psychotherapists, chaplains, and doctors have been known to report service members dealing with issues of homosexuality, according the Human Rights Campaign.

Such statistics and reports have led many to question the effectiveness of the policy. A bill was introduced into the House in 2005 to repeal "Don't Ask, Don't Tell." But it didn't make it out of committee.

President Barack Obama has stated that he does not support the "Don't Ask, Don't Tell" law.

Three years later, more than a hundred retired generals and admirals spoke out in favor of ending the discriminatory policy. And in 2010, President Barack Obama included the issue in his State of the Union address.

"We find unity in our incredible diversity, drawing on the promise enshrined in our Constitution: the notion that we are all created equal, that no matter who you are or what you look like, if you abide by the law you should be protected by it," he said. "We must continually renew this promise. . . . This year, I will work with Congress and our military to finally repeal the law that denies gay Americans the right to serve the country they love because of who they are."

FIND OUT MORE ON THE INTERNET

Time's Brief History of Gay's in the Military
www.time.com/time/nation/article/0,8599,1958246,00.html

Washington Post's "On Faith": Gays in the Military
newsweek.washingtonpost.com/onfaith/2010/02/gays_in_the_military/all.html

READ MORE ABOUT IT

McGowan, Jeffrey. *Major Conflict: One Gay Man's Life in the Don't-Ask-Don't-Tell Military*. New York: Broadway, 2005.

Shilts, Randy. *Conduct Unbecoming: Gays and Lesbians in the U.S. Military*. New York: St. Martin's Griffin, 2005.

chapter 4

Workplace Issues and Discrimination

As Chelsie Collins prepared for her prom, she had more on her mind than just finding a date. In fact, she had already found the perfect date. And that's when things got more complicated for the Alabama teen.

When Chelsie and her date, Lauren Farrington, announced their plans to attend the prom at Scottsboro High School, the news was not well-received. Dr. Judith Berry, the school superintendent, and the Scottsboro City Board of Education told them they were not permitted to attend together.

Rather than backing down to the discrimination, the Collins and Farrington families looked to the courts for assistance.

"The only reason they were not allowed to attend is that their sexual orientation was brought up," said Parker Edmiston, the attorney for the families.

Just hours before the event, the decision was made.

"John Graham, circuit court judge here in Jackson County ordered that the Scottsboro Board of Education (and) its administrators could not deny these girls attending their prom," Edmiston announced.

The decision was a blow to discrimination against gay and lesbian teens. But the news was not all good. The same year in Wisconsin, an out gay teen nominated for prom queen was not permitted to run for the title by his high school. Similar controversies continue to occur across the United States.

The history of discrimination in education and employment is highlighted with individuals standing up against injustice, beginning in 1957, when Dr. Franklin E. Kameny was fired by the U.S. Civil Service Commission from his post as an astronomer in the Army Map Service in Washington, D.C., because he was gay. He protested and argued his case in front of the U.S. Supreme Court in what has become known as one of the first major gay civil rights cases.

Brewing discontent with employment discrimination was one of the many factors contributing to the historic Stonewall riots, when thousands of people protested increasing intolerance of the gay community in 1969. "Before Stonewall, for most lesbians and gay men, being open on the

What's That Mean?

A *stigma* is a mark of disgrace or shame.

job was to invite an almost immediate dismissal and the **stigma** that came with it," said Bob Witeck, co-author of *Business Inside and Out*. "Workplaces were merely extended 'closets,' where gay men and lesbians concealed themselves completely, and made

Franklin Kameny formed a political partnership with Barbara Gittings, and together they launched some of the first gay activist movements.

very sure to cover their tracks, and bring opposite-sex dates to company occasions and parties."

Throughout the 1970s, individual businesses began making strides to ban workplace discrimination of gays and lesbians. And the first legislation aimed at protecting gay rights was introduced into the House of Representatives in 1975. Though it did not pass, it brought increasing attention on the issue.

In 1978, California State Senator John Biggs attempted a **ballot initiative** to ban gay teachers. "One third of San Francisco teachers are homosexual," Biggs announced at the time. "I assume most of them are seducing young boys in toilets."

The initiative failed, but **bias** and discrimination against homosexuals in the workplace continued. Currently, federal law provides protection against employment discrimination based on race, religion, sex, national origin, age, and disability. In 1994, the Employment Non-Discrimination Act (ENDA) was

What's That Mean?

A *ballot initiative* is an opportunity for citizens to vote for or against something. A number of U.S. states allow for this procedure, whereby citizens are able to draw up a petition for a proposed change in the law, which, if they can get enough signatures, will come before voters.

Bias is a tendency or preference toward a particular perspective or ideology, when the tendency interferes with the ability to be impartial, unprejudiced, or objective.

proposed in the U.S. Congress. Modeled after the Civil Rights Act of 1964 and the Americans with Disabilities Act, ENDA calls for extending federal protection to include discrimination based on sexual orientation and gender identity. The law would apply to government employees, but would not impact small businesses with fewer than fifteen employees, religious organizations, or the military.

Although it has been presented to Congress multiple times, ENDA had yet to pass as of June 24, 2009, when Representatives Barney Frank (Democrat-Massachusetts) and Ileana Ros-Lehtinen (Republican-Florida) introduced a new variation of ENDA to the 111th Congress. As of 2010, it continues to be legal in more than three dozen states to discriminate based on sexual orientation or gender identity.

Jacqueline Thomas experienced such discrimination when she was working a temporary job at a law firm. Though she never told colleagues she was gay, they made the assumption. Among other jibes and

Representative Barney Frank is an outspoken supporter of gay rights.

insults, she was told that AIDS existed because of people like her. And there was nothing she could do but leave the job.

"I always have to balance the financial consequences of coming out with the psychological consequences of not coming out," she said. "Although American workplace tolerance is increasing toward gays and lesbians, we still meet with some outright hostility. But harassment on the basis of sexual orientation has no place in our society."

EXTRA INFO

The Civil Rights Act of 1964 was a landmark piece of American legislation that outlawed unequal application of voter registration requirements and racial segregation in schools, at the workplace, and in all facilities that served the general public. Once the Act was implemented, its effects were far reaching and had tremendous long-term impacts on the whole country. It prohibited discrimination in public facilities, in government, and in employment. It became illegal to compel segregation of the races in schools, housing, or hiring.

The Americans with Disabilities Act of 1990 is a wide-ranging civil rights law that prohibits, under certain circumstances, discrimination based on disability. It gives similar protections against discrimination to Americans with disabilities as those covered in the Civil Rights Act of 1964.

Despite the shortcomings of employment law, popular opinion and other legal decisions continue to make strides toward ending discrimination against gay and lesbian people, whether in workplaces or at high school dances. In 2009, federal law was expanded to include gender identity and sexual orientation in hate crimes legislation. This means that

The Human Rights Campaign works to organize grassroots support for gay equality.

crimes committed against someone because of race, religion, gender, ethnicity, nationality, sexual orientation, gender identity, and disability can be federally prosecuted.

"Hiding one's sexual orientation takes work. But not coming out can take a terrible toll on a person's self-esteem and personal happiness," Thomas said.

Gay rights organizations have taken a grassroots approach to protesting homophobic organizations. Every year, the Human Rights Campaign releases a "Buying for Equality" list that encourages gay rights supporters to buy from businesses that have publicly stated employment policies that protect gay and lesbian employees. The organization also publishes a Corporate Equality Index, rating hundreds of the nation's biggest employers on their benefits to gay employees.

"Now that we have an unprecedented opportunity to effect dramatic change for our community, it is more important than ever that we keep our allies in this fight close at hand," said Joe Salmonese, president of the Human Rights Campaign Foundation. "We can help seize this opportunity with the economic choices we make. Each time we spend money, we support one or more companies. We need to support our community with these choices. . . . (Our guide) shows which corporations support our community—through nondiscrimination policies, equal family benefits, comprehensive healthcare, and employee support—and which do not."

Many states and government agencies also continue to move forward to provide the workplace protections that Dr. Franklin Kameny fought so hard to achieve. And on June 29, 2009, more than fifty years after his dismissal, he was finally vindicated. In a ceremony hosted by the Office of Personnel Management (OPM), the re-named department that had fired him five decades earlier, OPM Director John Berry formally apologized to Kameny on behalf of the U.S. government. The statement was met with a resounding, "Apology accepted!" from the aged Dr. Kameny, who also received the Theodore Roosevelt Award, the department's most prestigious honor.

"With the fervent passion of a true patriot, you did not resign yourself to your fate or quietly endure this wrong. With courage and strength, you fought back," Berry wrote in the official letter presented to Dr. Kameny. "Please accept our apology for the consequences of the previous policy of the United States government, and please accept the gratitude and appreciation of the United States Office of Personnel Management for the work you have done to fight discrimination."

FIND OUT MORE ON THE INTERNET

Anti-Gay Discrimination in Schools: Teaching Tolerance
www.tolerance.org/activity/anti-gay-discrimination-schools

Workplace Discrimination
civilliberty.about.com/od/gendersexuality/ig/Lesbian-and-Gay-Rights-101/Anti-Gay-Discrimination.htm

READ MORE ABOUT IT

Gold, Mitchell and Wendy Drucker. *Crisis: 40 Stories Revealing the Personal, Social, and Religious Pain and Trauma of Growing Up Gay in America.* Austin, Tex.: Greenleaf, 2008.

Human Rights Watch. *Hatred in the Hallways: Violence and Discrimination Against Lesbian, Gay, Bisexual and Transgender Students in U.S. Schools.* New York: Human Rights Watch, 2001.

BIBLIOGRAPHY

Alwood, Edward. *Straight News: Gays, Lesbians and the News Media.* New York: Columbia University Press, 1996.

American Psychiatric Association. *Diagnostic and Statistical Manual of Mental Disorders (3rd ed., Revised).* Washington, D.C.: American Psychiatric Association, 1987.

"Armed Forces: No to Matlovich," *Time*, September 29, 1975.

Discovery Health. Sexual Health Center. health.discovery.com/centers/sex/sexpedia/homosexuality.html.

Eskridge, William N. *Dishonorable Passions: Sodomy Laws in America, 1861-2003.* New York: Viking Adult, 2008.

Exodus International. www.exodusinternational.org.

Freedom to Marry. www.freedomtomarry.org.

Gay and Lesbian Alliance Against Defamation. www.glaad.org.

"Gay Marriage." *The Urban L Magazine*, September 29, 2009.

Hollie, Rashad. "Gay Prom: Lesbians Win Legal Right To Attend High School Prom." *NBC News Channel*, April 1, 2008.

The Kameny Papers. www.kamenypapers.org.

The Leadership Conference. www.civilrights.org.

Matthew Shepard Foundation. www.matthewshepard.org.

Moser, Bob. "Holy War." *Intelligence Report*, Spring 2005.

Obama, Barack. "Remarks by the President in State of the Union Address." Whitehouse.gov, January 27, 2010.

O'Keefe, Ed. "Eye Opener: Apology for Frank Kameny." *Washington Post*, June 29, 2009.

The Online Office of U.S. Congressman John Lewis. johnlewis.house. gov.

Rotondi, James. "Same-Sex Marriage: 'A Basic Civil Right'" *The Huffington Post,* December 2008.

Servicemembers Legal Defense Network. www.sldn.org.

Shilts, Randy. *And the Band Played On: Politics, People and the AIDS Epidemic.* New York: St. Martin's Griffin, 1987.

Shilts, Randy. *The Mayor of Castro Street: The Life and Times of Harvey Milk.* New York: St Martin's Griffin, 1998.

Singleton, Dave. "LGBT Leaders Age 50 + : What Does Stonewall Mean to You?" *AARP.org*, June 2009.

"The Thirty Years War: A timeline of the anti-gay movement." *Intelligence Report*, Spring 2005.

INDEX

ABOUT THE AUTHOR AND THE CONSULTANT

Jaime A. Seba's involvement in LGBT issues began in 2004, when she helped open the doors of the Pride Center of Western New York, which served a community of more than 100,000 people. As head of public education and outreach, she spearheaded one of the East Coast's first crystal methamphetamine awareness and harm reduction campaigns. She also wrote and developed successful grant programs through the Susan G. Komen Breast Cancer Foundation, securing funding for the region's first breast cancer prevention program designed specifically for gay, bisexual, and transgender women. Jaime studied political science at Syracuse University before switching her focus to communications with a journalism internship at the *Press & Sun-Bulletin* in Binghamton, New York, in 1999. She is currently a freelance writer based in Seattle.

James T. Sears specializes in research in lesbian, gay, bisexual, and transgender issues in education, curriculum studies, and queer history. His scholarship has appeared in a variety of peer-reviewed journals and he is the author or editor of twenty books and is the Editor of the *Journal of LGBT Youth*. Dr. Sears has taught curriculum, research, and LGBT-themed courses in the departments of education, sociology, women's studies, and the honors college at several universities, including: Trinity University, Indiana University, Harvard University, Penn State University, the College of Charleston, and the University of South Carolina. He has also been a Research Fellow at Center for Feminist Studies at the University of Southern California, a Fulbright Senior Research Southeast Asia Scholar on sexuality and culture, a Research Fellow at the University of Queensland, a consultant for the J. Paul Getty Center for Education and the Arts, and a Visiting Research Lecturer in Brazil. He lectures throughout the world.